T0194903

Brown House, Blue House

Brown House, Blue House

Samiliah Peasah-Boateng,
Bernard & Solomon Boateng

WestBow Press books may be ordered through booksellers or by contacting:

WestBow Press
A Division of Thomas Nelson & Zondervan
1663 Liberty Drive
Bloomington, IN 47403
www.westbowpress.com
1 (866) 928-1240

ISBN: 978-1-9736-3027-2 (sc)
ISBN: 978-1-9736-3130-9 (e)

Library of Congress Control Number: 2018907000

Print information available on the last page.

WestBow Press rev. date: 1/10/2019

WESTBOW
PRESS®
A DIVISION OF THOMAS NELSON
& ZONDERVAN

To my boys Bernard and Solomon.
May you always feel loved; wherever you live.

Love you lots,
Mommy

My mommy and daddy have two houses. My Daddy lives at the brown house and Mommy lives at the blue house. My brother Solomon and I have one (1) house, two (2) houses? How about you?

On Mondays, we live at the blue house. Mommy drives us to school. We get to eat breakfast at the blue house and sleep there too. After school Daddy picks us up and we are off to the brown house. Do you have one (1) house or two (2) houses? Brown house, blue house how about you?

On Tuesdays, we live at the brown house. Daddy wakes us up with hugs and kisses. He says, in a funny voice "My bob-boys," and we say, "Yes Big Daddy." Daddy is funny, he always makes us laugh when he calls us that at the brown house. At the brown house, we wake up, brush our teeth, take a bath, get dressed, eat breakfast and off to school we go. Daddy picks us up after school and we go back to the brown house again. Do you have one (1) house or two (2) houses? Brown house, blue house how about you?

On Wednesdays, we are still at the brown house with Daddy. We have more fun and Daddy takes us to school again. After school, Mommy picks us up and off we go to the blue house. At the blue house we do homework, Mommy signs our planners and we eat dinner. At the blue house Mommy reads us bedtime stories, and we pray together. The blue house is fun too. Do you have one (1) house or two (2) houses? Brown house, blue house how about you?

On Thursdays, my little brother Solomon
and I, wake up bright and early. Mommy
has to go to work early so she drops
us off at the daycare center. We eat
breakfast at the daycare, and the daycare
van takes us to school. I like the daycare.
We have lots of friends at the daycare..

On Fridays, Mommy takes us to school. She says, when she drops us off, "don't forget boys, today is fun Friday." Yeah! We shout. We like fun Fridays, Mommy takes us to the movies and dinner on fun Fridays. After school Mommy picks us up and off we go to the movies. At the movies Mommy buys us snacks like popcorn and juice. We always have fun at the movies. After the movies off we go to dinner. I like dinner because we eat and talk with Mommy at dinner. Do you have one (1) house or two (2) houses? Brown house, blue house how about you?

On Saturdays, we sleep in. Mommy says don't get up until its light outside or noon. Solomon and I sleep in, because it has been a long week at the brown house and the blue house. On Saturdays, we stay home and clean our room with Mommy. Mommy doesn't like messy rooms. We eat breakfast, take a bath, and get dress quickly. Because Daddy is coming to pick us up, and we are off to the brown house, the fun house. We spend time with Daddy at the park. We swing, run, and play tennis with Daddy. Mommy picks us up at the brown house. Do you have one (1) house or two (2) houses? Brown house, blue house how about you?

On Sundays, we wake up and watch cartoons until Mommy wake up. When Mommy wakes up, its pancakes time! Mommy makes pancakes on Sundays with turkey bacon. Do you like pancakes? I love pancakes. After breakfast we brush our teeth, take a bath, get dress, and off to church we go. We like church, we learn and eat snacks there. We have a busy schedule Monday thru Sunday, how about you? Do you have one (1) house or two (2) houses? Brown house, blue house how about you?

Printed in the United States
By Bookmasters